The

WISDOM

of the Celts

Compiled and Translated by Thor Ewing

edda uk
Cambridge
2005

For my son Caradoc, who was not
born when this book was begun

Thor Ewing

The Wisdom of the Celts
Published by edda uk ltd.
Cambridge

© edda uk 2005
© Translation of Poems Thor Ewing
© Introduction Thor Ewing

Design: Helgi Hilmarsson

ISBN 1-904945-02-3

Contents

Acknowledgements

I should like to thank Dr William Mahon and Dr Marged Haycock for their invaluable help both with the translations and with aspects of the introduction, and Professor Patrick Sims-Williams and Dr Simon James for reading and advising on the introduction. Special thanks are due to Dr Jenny Rowland, for giving up her time at short notice to help with some final questions. Between them, these scholars have saved me from a variety of errors. I have tried to incorporate their suggestions wherever possible, but if I have sometimes failed to follow their good advice I hope they will understand. Responsibility for any errors is of course mine alone.

I should also like to thank my wife for her support without which this book would not have been possible, my father for his continued enthusiasm, and Björn for putting me up to it and patiently awaiting its delivery.

Thor Ewing
Shropshire 2004

Publisher's Note

The Wisdom series is intended for the general reader. These books are intended to open up a little window on the past through which readers may catch a tantalising glimpse of ancient cultures. We hope that this will encourage people to go further and get to know these cultures and their histories better. Every effort has been made to create books that readers will find interesting and enjoyable, applying the highest standards in both the production of the text and the design and presentation.

By comparing the books in the Wisdom series, readers will see how the same idea often turns up at different times and places, only dressed in different clothing. The Celts chose other ways to express themselves than the Romans; the men of the North do not always speak like those of the Mediterranean. In many cases it is the literary tradition of a particular culture that determines the form of the text and sets its own mark on a familiar idea.

By bringing these classic texts to a modern audience in a new version, we hope that readers will gain an insight into the glories of the past, and that these glories will live on to inspire new generations of readers, both young and old.

THREES

hree signs of wisdom:
Patience;
Memory;
Foresight.

hree signs of foolishness:
Strife;
Squabbling;
Dependency.

Three signs of a cheat:
Spreading rumours;
Spiteful pranks;
Jokes which raise a blush.

hree signs of passion:
Sighing;
Flirting;
Visiting.

Three locks hide secrets:
Shame;
Silence;
Inwardness.

Three keys unlock thoughts:
Drunkenness;
Trust;
Love.

13

Three lamps
        light every darkness:
Truth;
Nature;
Knowledge.

hree glories of speech:
Steadiness;
Wisdom;
Brevity.

 hree silences better
than speech:
Silence during teaching;
Silence during music;
Silence during the sermon.

 hree needed for justice:
Reason;
Deliberation;
Conscience.

Three needed for judgment:
Wisdom;
Insight;
Knowledge.

hree ranks
ruin a nation through deceit:
A deceitful leader;
A deceitful historian;
A deceitful judge.

hree are best for a leader:
Justice;
Peace;
An army.

Three are worst for a leader:
Laziness;
Treachery;
Bad counsel.

hree downfalls of a nation:
A lying leader;
A false judge;
A lustful priest.

Three downfalls of any leader:
Falsehood;
Extortion;
Murder.

hree
    that are hardest to talk with:
A leader with his spoils;
And a foreigner in armour;
And a tenant
        backed by a big landlord.

hree drops of a wedded wife:
Dropping blood;
Dropping tears;
Dropping sweat.

hree grins
            worse than sorrow:
The grin of snow in melt;
The grin your woman gives you
        after bedding another man;
The grin of a dog pouncing.

hree joys with remorse:
The wooer's;
The thief's;
The tell-tale's.

hree 'fews' better
         than 'manys':
A few fine words;
A few cows at grass;
A few friends at drink.

hree sisters of Youth:
Wantonness;
Beauty;
Generosity.

hree sisters of Age:
Sighing;
Chastity;
Ugliness.

hree sisters of Falsehood:
'Perhaps . . .'
'Maybe . . .'
'Surely . . .'

hree brothers of Fear:
'Hush!'
'Shush!'
'Listen!'

Three slight strands
        that best support the world:
The strand of milk from udder to pail;
The strand of green corn on the ground;
The strand of thread in a woman's hand.

There deaths better than life:
The death of the salmon;
The death of the fattened pig;
The death of the robber.

hree living
            that shed the dead:
Deer shedding antlers;
Wood shedding leaves;
Cattle shedding hair.

hree dead
          are bought with life:
The Apple-tree;
The Hazel-tree;
The Holy Grove.

hree renewers of the world:
A woman's womb;
A cow's udder;
A smith's anvil.

FROM THE RED
BOOK OF HERGEST

Close-set

Close-set the warriors,
  close-branched the ash,
Ducks on the lake,
  sand-white the wave;

Stronger than a hundred
  is the heart's counsel.

ong the night,
gloomy the marshes;
Usual, uproar at meetings;

The wretch will not
agree with the good.

Long the night,
   gloomy the fells,
Whistling wind
   in the tops of the trees;

Ill-nature will not
   betray the blameless.

 aplings the birches,
   green-tipped;
It frees my foot
   from its snare,

That I tell no lad a secret.

aplings the oaks
in the grove;
It frees my foot
from its fetter,

That I tell no lass a secret.

aplings the oaks
   all leafy;
It frees my foot
   from its bonds,

That I tell no blabber a secret.

 aplings the briars,
  bearing berries;
Not the blackbird
  on her nest

Nor the liar are ever silent.

Rain outside,
  drenching the bracken,
White sea shingle,
  the edge of foam;
Bright is the light
  of reason for Man.

ain outside,
  warmth within,
Yellow gorse,
  withering cow-parsley;
Lord God,
  why did you make the coward?

ain outside,
  drenching my hair,
The weak lamenting,
  steep the hill;

Pallid the sea,
  salt the brine.

 ain outside,
  drenching the sea,
Whistling wind
    in the tops of the reeds;

Each feat is widowed
    if there be no skill.

51

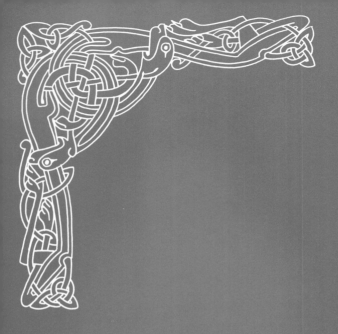

Snow on the Fells

Snow on the fells,
  everywhere white,
The raven's custom is to sing;

No good will come
  of sleeping too long.

now on the fells,
  the gully white,
In the rush of wind,
  trees bending;

Many a couple may love
  Though they are never united.

now on the fells,
  drifting in the wind
Broad the moonlight,
  the dock-leaves grey;

A wretch is rarely
  without a lawsuit.

Snow on the fells,
   the stag running,
Usual, brave men in Britain;

The outcast has want of his wits.

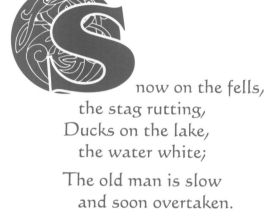

now on the fells,
   the stag rutting,
Ducks on the lake,
   the water white;

The old man is slow
   and soon overtaken.

 now on the fells,
  the stag roaming,
The heart smiles
  on what it loves;

Though I am spun a tale,
  I know shame no matter where.

now on the fells,
  sand-white scree,
The fish in the ford,
  the cave's shelter,

The harsh shall be hateful.

Snow on the fells,
   the stag fleeing,
Usual, for a king,
   a shining weapon,

And to mount
   by the saddle-bow.

now on the fells,
    the stag hunched,
Much have I said,
    as I know;

It is not like a summer's day.

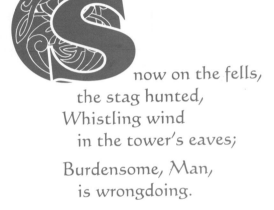now on the fells,
the stag hunted,
Whistling wind
in the tower's eaves;

Burdensome, Man,
is wrongdoing.

Snow on the fells,
   the stag leaping,
Whistling wind
   on the white high wall;

Usual, beauty in stillness.

Snow on the fells,
   the stag on the land,
Whistling wind
   on the top of the roof;

Evil cannot hide, no matter where.

Snow on the fells,
  the stag on the shore;
Old age will know
  the loss of youth;

A man is imprisoned
  by failing sight.

Snow on the fells,
the stag in the grove,
Coal-black the raven,
swift the roebuck,

A healthy freeman,
he seldom will moan.

Snow on the fells,
   the stag in the rushes,
Cold the marshes,
   the mead in the vat;

Usual, that the wounded moan.

Snow on the fells,
    the tower-breast flecked,
The beast seeking shelter;

Woe on the wife
    who takes a bad man.

Snow on the fells,
   red the tops of the pear-trees,
Close-set and angry
   the spear-points;

Oh, the longing
   for my brothers!

Snow on the fells,
  swift the wolf,
Prowling the edge
  of the wastes;
Usual, all hardships
  on the wretch.

Snow on the fells,
   the stag not slow,
Rain, falling from the sky;
Sorrow brings
   utter hopelessness.

Snow on the fells,
the deer speedy,
Waves wash
the edge of the shore;

Cunning hides its purpose.

Snow on the fells,
   the stag in the glen,
Soft the summer,
   still the lake,

Grey-bearded the frost;
   the bold on the edge.

Snow on the fells,
the goose-breast flecked;
Strong my arm
and my shoulder;
I hope I shan't live
till a hundred!

Snow on the fells,
  the reed-tips bare,
Branch-tops bent,
  the fish in the flood;

Where there's no learning,
  there'll be no skill.

Snow on the fells,
   the fish in the ford,
The withered stag
   seeks a sheltered valley;

Longing for the dead
   can do no good.

Snow on the fells,
   the stag in the wood;
The fortunate shall not
   go by foot;

The coward causes
   many wounds.

Snow on the fells,
  the stag on the slopes,
Whistling wind
  in the tops of the ash-trees;

A third foot for an old man,
  his stick.

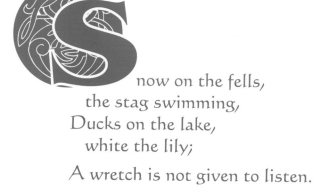

now on the fells,
the stag swimming,
Ducks on the lake,
white the lily;

A wretch is not given to listen.

now on the fells,
  the hens' feet red;
The brook is shallow
  where it babbles;

Big words only add
  to the shame.

Snow on the fells,
   swift the stag;
I little care
   for things of the world;

Warning the unlucky
   can do no good.

Snow on the fells,
   a fleece of white;
A dear cousin's face
   becomes unfriendly

If you call on him too often.

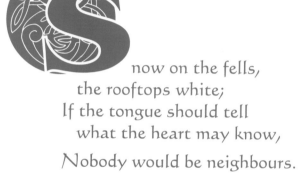

now on the fells,
the rooftops white;
If the tongue should tell
what the heart may know,

Nobody would be neighbours.

Snow on the fells,
   the break of day;
The sad all sick,
   the poor half-naked;

Usual, all hardships on the fool.

Usual

sual,
   the wind from the south;
Usual, treasures in the church;
Usual, that the weakling is skinny;
Usual, that a man asks the news;
Usual, that the fosterling is pampered.

sual,
　　the wind from the east;
Usual, that the bighead is proud;
Usual, the blackbird
　　among the thorns;
Usual, after pride, lamentation;
Usual, that ravens
　　get meat in the wood.

sual,
  the wind from the north;
Usual, that girls are sweet;
Usual, a handsome man in Gwynedd;
Usual, that the prince gives a feast;
Usual, after drink, befuddlement.

sual,
    the wind from the sea;
Usual, the flowing of the tide;
Usual, that the sow breeds lice;
Usual, that pigs dig for earth-nuts.

Usual,
    the wind from the fells;
Usual, a bumpkin in the country;
Usual, to get thatch in the marshes;
Usual, a priest bred on milk;
Usual are leaves, saplings and trees.

The Wisdom of the Celts

Few ancient cultures inspire such fascination or controversy as the Celts. Even the most basic question 'who were the Celts?' depends on who is looking and where they look: They are the blue-painted hordes that defied the might of Rome; they are the white robed druids with the golden sickles; they are the hermit monks who travelled wherever the breath of God would guide their frail skin boats. But whether as dauntless warriors, prescient druids or windblown monks, the Celts have a special place in the minds of many.

This multiplicity of meanings follows the Celts throughout their history. The word 'Celt' is used by the Ancient Greeks and Romans of peoples who lived in mainland Europe; Strabo places 'Celtica' between Iberia and the Rhine, adding that the island of Britain lies opposite its north shore. Yet today the word 'Celt' is used of peoples living in, or originating in, Britain and Ireland.

In the eighteenth century the Welsh scholar Lhuyd drew public attention to the similarity between the language of the ancient Gauls and modern Welsh and Irish. The term 'Celtic' was swiftly applied to a group of similar languages, made up of Gaelic Celtic languages (which were still spoken in Scotland, Ireland and Man) and Brythonic Celtic languages (spoken in Wales, and Brittany, and then stuttering to a stop in Cornwall). A new Celtic identity was born, which pitted Scots, Irish and Welsh against the English, who came to be seen as the very antithesis of Celticness.

In the mid-nineteenth century, excavations at the Continental sites of Hallstatt (Austria) and La Tène (Switzerland) revealed a thriving and distinctive prehistoric culture. Artefacts in styles similar to the finds from these sites were discovered across much of Europe, and these were quickly claimed as the products of the ancient Celtic world. The Celts were envisaged as a people who, originating in central Europe, swept all before them to settle over a vast swathe of land from the Black Sea to the Atlantic. In the late nineteenth century, archaeologists believed that they had found firm evidence for the Celtic invasion and settlement of Britain in the pre-Roman Iron Age. This Celtic population was believed to have later been driven out by the Anglo-Saxon invaders who settled England after the Romans, and to have survived only in the mountain fastnesses of Scotland and Wales.

This picture of Celtic prehistory is now no longer trusted. Cultures can spread without the need for large-scale invasion and settlement, and the Celtic expansion is seen less as the history of a people, more as the history of a culture. The population of Britain in the Celtic Iron Age came of much the same stock as it had in the Bronze Age and before, and the inhabitants of Britain today are often descended from the same remote forebears. Not only this, but the same regional stereotypes can hold true today as did two thousand years ago. The modern British nations, whether Welsh, Scottish or English, can all trace their ancestry in part to the pre-Celtic inhabitants of the island.

We cannot know to what extent Iron Age Britons saw themselves as belonging to the same culture as the Continental Celts. But Caesar writes that the coastal peoples of Britain had come from Europe, and we can recognise some of the same tribes on both sides of the Channel. Whether in Britain or in Gaul, these tribal groupings probably represent the territories of a small warrior elite, whose ethnic origins may have been relatively mixed, but who shared a common tribal identity and a common Celtic culture.

Caesar also writes that the druids, the powerful Celtic priesthood, originated in Britain, and that Celts from Gaul who wanted to train as druids came to Britain for their education. There are mythological links too; the god Lugus, worshipped in Lyons, is known from myths recorded in medieval Wales and Ireland. So, British and Continental cultures were clearly closely interwoven in pre-Roman times. Indeed, the cultural and religious heart of Celtic Gaul appears to have been British in origin.

There are real differences from region to region throughout the ancient Celtic world; Britain and Ireland share aspects of a common 'island' culture, distinct from the rest of Europe, and there are important variations even within Britain. These cultures are separate, but linked. The Iron Age Irish are linked to the British are linked to the Celts of northern Gaul and so on. Each is distinct, but akin to its neighbours within a single linguistic community.

One of the most distinctive features of Celtic Britain and Ireland is its art. This may take its cue from European Celtic art, but from the third century BC onwards, a unique and fascinating insular art form develops. Often quite abstract, it makes use of a few simple curves and spirals to produce elaborate designs, which appear to grow and spread organically across the decorated surface. The overall composition may or may not show symmetry, and appears to be formed less through logical progression as through sudden associations and lateral leaps. But despite the free form of the overall pattern, the designs are governed by a complex geometry and drawn using compasses. This art form is perhaps brought to its height in the exquisite mirror-back patterns of pre-Roman Britain. Towards the end of the Roman era, Celtic forms re-assert themselves in British art and, blended with a variety of other influences, they continue well into the early medieval period.

It is not unreasonable to imagine that Celtic literature may have enjoyed a similar renaissance at this time; some of the earliest poetry known today was composed for the warlords of later post-Roman Britain. Thus, the themes and interests of the island Celts may perhaps be heard in the early writings of their cultural heirs, which sometimes seem to describe a society not far removed from that of pre-Roman times, and which preserve stories of gods who are honoured on Roman-era monuments. It is through these writings, poems and sagas, myths and legends, from early medieval Wales and Ireland, that we get our closest glimpse of the mindset of an ancient culture. But this is also the voice of a Christian people, and if there are similarities between the early medieval and ancient Celts, there are also marked differences. The literature of the medieval Celts is the product of their own world; if it also catches the sound of an earlier world it is as an echo that has yet to fade.

Of all the abstract symbols in the Iron Age art of Britain and Ireland, perhaps the most common and most quintessentially Celtic is the 'triskele'. This motif remained in Celtic art of the Middle Ages, and a somewhat cumbersome triskele, made up of armoured legs, is still the badge of the Isle of Man to this day. It sums up the Celtic sense of sinuous poise and perfect balance, dividing the circle into equal and gracefully shaped parts. The balance and the curves are Celtic, but most of all the triskele is Celtic in its use of threes.

For the island Celts were fascinated by threeness, which appears in all aspects of their culture. This sense of threeness is nowhere better expressed than in the Welsh and Irish lists of Threes. Some of these Threes (commonly known in English as Triads) are clearly very old. No doubt, the form goes back to the earliest times; it has the beauty and power of utter simplicity, which also makes it an unbeatable mnemonic device. And its effect is not lessened because we still think in threes today; what other number of 'deaths that are better than life' could hold our attention? So whilst there are occasional Fours and other numbers, they are always less memorable for their deviation from the norm.

The Roman Cato writes that the Celts valued nothing so highly as glory and wit. More recently, they have gained something of a reputation for dreaminess, and it may be a surprise to find a wry almost bitter humour underlying some of the Threes and other wisdom verses in this book. But this hard-edged humour is very much a part of the real Celtic worldview. It stems from the earthy rootedness of the poems, from a clear eye that sees things for what they are, and a tongue that calls a spade by its name. Celtic mist and twilight are born of nineteenth-century Romanticism, and have no place in the gritty and often violent world of our ancient and medieval Celtic forebears.

Although there are proverbial threes in Welsh manu-scripts, most are principally concerned with history or law, or else with characters and events in medieval story and tradition. Welsh gnomic wisdom is more often embedded in poetic sequences where a proverb makes up one line of each three-line verse or englyn. The most sophisticated of these sequences are often held together by repeated imagery drawn from the natural world.

The natural imagery adds resonance and weight, giving each maxim a specific symbolic context in a universal world; it is as if the maxim itself becomes as real as the running stag, the growing sapling or the falling rain. And beside the universal truth of the maxim, the running stag comes to signify all running stags; the falling rain to represent the universal truth that rain will fall. This combination of image and maxim seems to say that, just as the stag will run so the outcast must have his wits about him, or whatever the proverb may be. The association of image and maxim is governed by the same flash of insight, the same lateral association, as appears to direct the Celtic art of an earlier age.

Moreover, the poetic sequences each suggest a specific poetic voice (some are associated with tales of the semi-legendary exile Llywarch the Old) and the natural imagery can illustrate the landscape the sage is looking at; it often suggests a human condition, perhaps one which the imagined speaker finds relevant, and which is also reflected in the proverb itself. Each verse is carefully weighted to speak not only a universal truth, but one with specific relevance to the speaker, so that each casts its own light on the scenario, and when they are read together they begin to reveal his position: is the poet of the 'Rain Outside' verses unable to take the revenge he feels he must? Is this the explanation of the fetters, bonds and snares in the 'Saplings' verses? Is the voice that raven-like croaks the 'Snow on the Fells' verses living as an outlaw, or as an aged dispossessed chieftain?

These Welsh sequences are preserved in a manuscript called The Red Book of Hergest, after the colour of the binding and the place near Kington, Herefordshire, where it was once kept. Most scholars would date the poems in their present form to the twelfth or perhaps the eleventh century, though changes and additions may have been made at any time before they were written down, some time around 1400. But much of the material they contain, and indeed their distinctive poetic form of proverbs set in the context of the natural world, may be much older, so that these poems may preserve elements of a distinctively Celtic culture.

I have chosen to give two sequences in their entirety: the first, of eleven verses, begins with the words 'Close-set the warriors' and contains three tightly-linked internal sequences beginning 'Long the night', 'Saplings' and 'Rain outside'; all thirty-six verses of the second sequence begin 'Snow on the fells'. I have also chosen the first five verses from a third sequence, each line beginning with the word 'Usual'; further verses which form part of the same sequence in the manuscript are different in style and may be later additions.

The Irish Threes are principally drawn from four major medieval collections (found in The Yellow Book of Lecan, The Great Book of Lecan, The Book of Ballymote and The Book of Huí Maine), where they are listed together in much the way they are here. Of the hundreds of triads gathered in these manuscripts, the scholar Kuno Meyer remarked in his edition of 1906, "it is but a small portion of the large number of triads scattered throughout early Irish literature."

Finally, I should note that I have occasionally tweaked the literal meaning of a verse to keep its essential truth for the modern world. Thus for instance, where the Irish triad condemns a king for killing his family to get to the throne, modern leaders are more likely to have other skeletons in their closets. In the main however, I have tried to remain close to the original texts as presented and understood in the seminal editions of Kenneth Jackson and Kuno Meyer.

Further reading

Early Celtic literature in translation:
Joseph P. Clancy *Medieval Welsh Poems* Dublin (Four Courts Press) 2003
David Green & Frank O'Connor *A Golden Treasury of Irish Poetry: AD 600 – 1200* London (Macmillan) 1967, Dingle, Co. Kerry (Brandon) 1990
Kenneth Jackson *A Celtic Miscellany* London (Routledge and Kegan Paul) 1951, Harmondsworth (Penguin) 1973 and subsequent reprints
John T Koch (ed.) *The Celtic Heroic Age* Malden, Massachusetts (Celtic Studies) 1997, 4th edition 2003
Gerard Murphy *Early Irish Lyrics: Eighth to Twelfth Centuries* Oxford (OUP) 1956, Dublin (Four Courts Press) 1998
Jenny Rowland *Early Welsh Saga Poetry: A Study and Edition of the Englynion* Cambridge (Brewer) 1990

Other books about the Celts:
Barry Cunliffe *The Celts: A Very Short Introduction* Oxford (OUP) 2003
John Haywood *Historical Atlas of the Celtic World* London (Thames and Hudson) 2001
Ruth and Vincent Megaw *Celtic Art* London (Thames and Hudson) 1989, new edition 2001

Sources for this book:
Kenneth Jackson *Early Welsh Gnomic Poems* Cardiff (University of Wales Press) 1935
Kenneth Jackson *Studies in Early Celtic Nature Poetry* Cambridge (CUP) 1935, Felinfach (Llanerch) 1995
Kuno Meyer *The Triads of Ireland* Dublin & London (Royal Irish Academy, Todd Lecture Series vol.13) 1906